This book belongs to:

_____

FLORA AND THE FERN

Alyssa K. Arseneau

Printed in the United States by

CreateSpace, An Amazon.com Company

Arseneau, Alyssa Flora and the Fern

SUMMARY: A young girl lives in a world where there are no plants or animals. She discovers a fern and is introduced to the intricate world of nature.

ISBN-13: 978-1511512374

ISBN-10: 1511512377

[1. Apocalypse-Science Fiction

2. Nature-Science 3. Adventure-Fiction]

www.CreateSpace.com/5308682

www.FloraAndTheFern.com

For all those who find it hard to finish what they have started,
and those who helped me continue along my own rocky trail.
We are all connected---let's change the world.

*"From my rotting body flowers shall grow and I am in them
and that is eternity."*

-Edvard Munch

PART ONE

FLORA FINDS A FRIEND

THIS IS FLORA, SHE IS
THE ONLY ONE LEFT IN
THE WORLD

AGE: TWELVE
ADDRESS: IT DOES NOT
EXIST. FLORA LIVES IN A
POST APOCALYPTIC WORLD
WHERE THERE IS ALMOST
NOTHING LEFT
HER FATHER: GONE
HER MOTHER: GONE
LIKES: WIND
DISLIKES: ROCKS
PROBLEM: THERE ARE MORE
ROCKS THAN WIND IN HER
WORLD

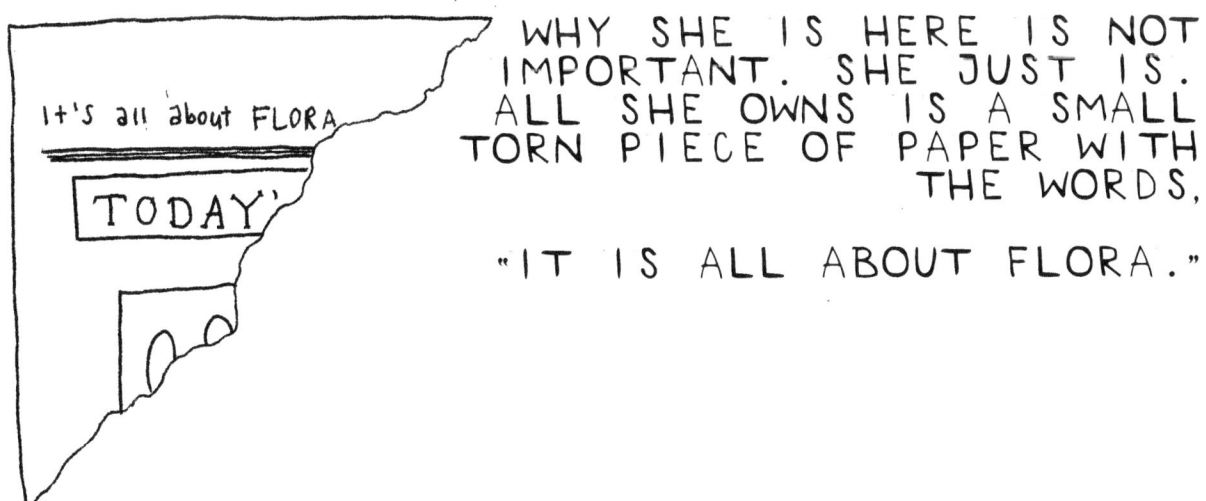

It's all about FLORA

TODAY'

WHY SHE IS HERE IS NOT
IMPORTANT. SHE JUST IS.
ALL SHE OWNS IS A SMALL
TORN PIECE OF PAPER WITH
THE WORDS,

"IT IS ALL ABOUT FLORA."

FLORA FLIPS OVER ROCKS EVERYDAY AND
WAITS FOR THE OCCASIONAL GUST OF WIND.
THERE WAS NOTHING ELSE TO DO

because everything ended.

THE LAND SHE LIVES IN IS BARREN. ALL
SHE COULD SEE FOR MILES WERE ROCKS.
GREY ROCKS, WHITE ROCKS, BLACK ROCKS AND
SOMETIMES DEADLY SPIKE ROCKS, WHICH SHE
CAREFULLY AVOIDED. HILL AFTER HILL.
ONLY ROCKS. FLORA WASN'T SURE HOW FAR
SHE HAD EVER TRAVELED BECAUSE
EVERYTHING LOOKED THE SAME SINCE THE
END.

FLORA PRETENDS THE WIND WILL CARRY HER AWAY TO A MAGICAL LAND. IT NEVER HAPPENS, BUT SHE ENJOYS THE WAY IT BLOWS THROUGH HER HAIR. SHE WONDERS IF TURNING OVER ROCKS WILL EVER MAKE A DIFFERENCE.

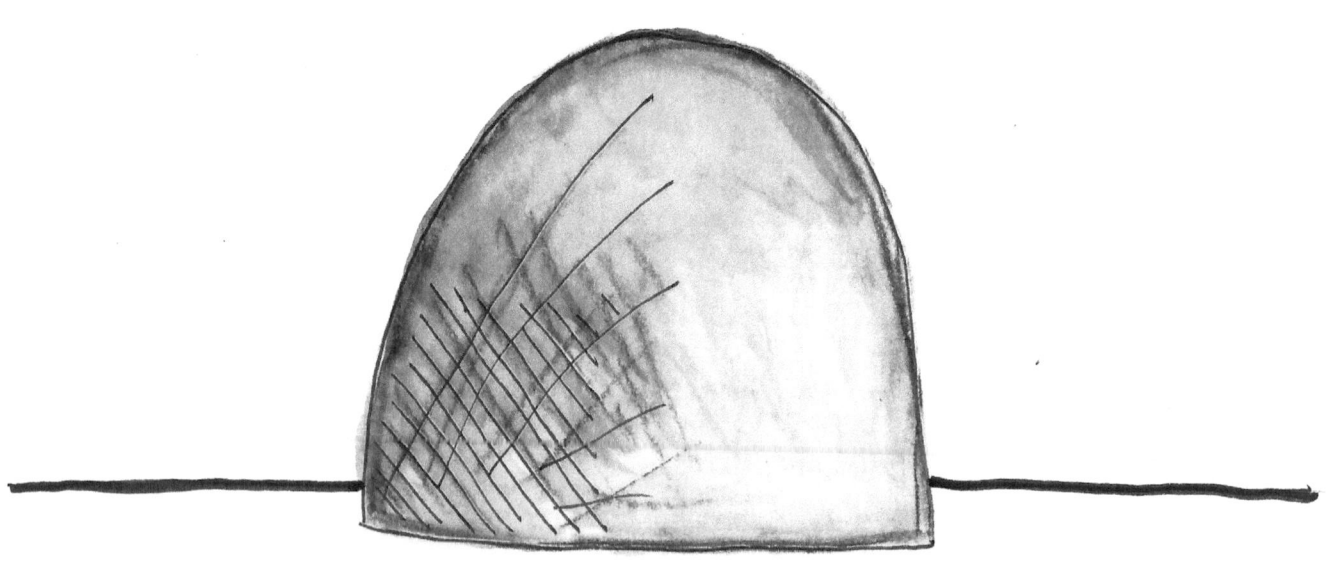

ON NO DAY IN PARTICULAR FLORA
TURNED OVER A ROCK THAT HAD ALWAYS
BEEN THERE. UNDERNEATH IT WAS
SOMETHING SPECIAL, SHE CARRIED ON
WITHOUT NOTICING BECAUSE NOTHING
DIFFERENT NORMALLY HAPPENED.

WAIT, THAT ROCK WAS.........

GREEN

SHE RAN BACK AS FAST AS SHE COULD AND
THERE IT WAS. NOT A GREEN ROCK AT ALL,
BUT GROWING OUT OF THE CRACKS,

A YOUNG SWORD FERN

a fiddlehead

SHE RETURNED EVERYDAY TO VISIT THE
LITTLE FERN. SOON, THE FERN WAS NO
LONGER LITTLE, BUT BIG AND BEAUTIFUL.
HER WORLD SEEMED MORE BEAUTIFUL TOO.

FLORA SAT AND
WATCHED AS THE
FERN'S FILIGREE

FLOURISHED

IN THE

SUNLIGHT

FLORA WAS CONTENT
BEING IN THE PRESENCE
OF THE FERN UNTIL,
ONE AFTERNOON,
THEY WERE INTERRUPTED
BY AN *UNEXPECTED*
VISITOR.

PART TWO

FIRSTS
FOR FLORA

THIS IS HARLIE

SPECIES: SUPERB
FAIRY WREN
ADDRESS: THE GREAT
PINK SILK TREE
HUSBAND: HE IS ONE
WIFE: HE HAS ONE
BORN: SOUTHEASTERN
AUSTRALIA IN THE
LUSH UNDERGROWTH
PROBLEM: EVERYTHING
ENDED IN AUSTRALIA
TOO SO HE HAD TO
FIND A NEW HOME AND
GET USED TO IT OR
HIS WHOLE FAMILY
WOULD DIE

FLORA WAS EXCITED TO SEE THE BIRD. HE
WOULD BE A NEW FRIEND. SHE KNEW HE
WOULD ALSO APPRECIATE SITTING WITH
HER FERN. THEN, SHE PANICKED. HARLIE
DID NOT COME TO MAKE FRIENDS, HE CAME
TO TAKE HER FERN. FLORA TRIED TO
SCARE HIM AWAY, BUT THE BIRD SNATCHED
HER FERN AND FLEW OFF.

FLORA HAD NEVER FELT MORE AWFUL. SHE
WAS FULL OF ANGER. THEN SHE FELT A
NEW FEELING,

curiosity.

SHE DECIDED SHE WOULD FOLLOW THE BIRD,
GET HER FERN BACK AND HAVE

revenge.

SO SHE BEGAN TO WALK, BUT LIKE A GUST OF WIND, THE BIRD WAS GONE. SHE WAS ON HER WAY TO GIVING UP AND THEN SOMETHING CAUGHT HER EYE. A SPORE. SHE HAD SEEN ONE BEFORE, SO SHE PICKED IT UP.

SHE CONTINUED TO WALK. HER WORLD BEGAN TO LOOK DIFFERENT, ALMOST LIKE SHE ENTERED A NEW PART OF THE LAND SHE HAD NEVER FOUND BEFORE. THE ROCKS SEEMED TO BE DISAPPEARING. SHE CONTINUED ON, HER CURIOSITY STRONGER THAN HER FEAR.

SHE CAME UPON A WALL SHE HAD NEVER
SEEN BEFORE. IF SHE WAS EVER GOING
TO FIND HER FERN SHE KNEW SHE HAD TO
CLIMB OVER IT.
AND THAT IS WHAT SHE DID.

SHE DID NOT KNOW IT, BUT SHE WAS
CLIMBING INTO A PLACE UNTOUCHED BY
THE END. THE ONLY REASON SHE COULD
SEE THIS PLACE WAS BECAUSE OF THE
SPORE THAT SAT IN HER POCKET. IT HAD
MAGICAL POWERS.

SHE REACHED THE TOP AND JUMPED. AS
SHE HIT THE GROUND, SHE WAS STARTLED
BY SOMETHING UNDER HER FEET. THE
GROUND WAS NO LONGER COVERED IN
SAND AND ROCKS, BUT SOIL AND GRASS.
THIS WORLD WAS COLORFUL.

FLORA WAS GETTING LOST IN THE
SQUISHY, MUSHY, LUXURIOUS FLOOR UNTIL
SHE HEARD A VOICE CALL OUT,

"COME WITH ME"

PART THREE
FLORA FORGETS

SHE HAD NOT HEARD ANOTHER SOUND IN AGES. THIS VOICE BELONGED TO THE BIRD! HE WAS BEAUTIFUL UP CLOSE. SHE IGNORED HIS BEAUTY AND SHOUTED, "WHU... WHE..." STUMBLING OVER HER FIRST WORDS, "WHERE IS MY FERN?"

"THE FERN IS NOT YOURS, BUT BELONGS TO ALL ON THIS EARTH," SAID THE BIRD.

"OKAY, THEN WHERE IS **THE** FERN?" SHE SAID, ANNOYED.

"COME WITH ME AND I WILL SHOW YOU."

SHE THOUGHT,

WHY SHOULD I HAVE TO GO WITH THIS BIRD? I FOUND THE FERN FIRST! IT IS MINE.

THE BIRD CLEARED HIS THROAT,

"IN CASE YOU WERE WONDERING, MY NAME IS CHARLIE PARKER. YOU CAN CALL ME HARLIE. I AM A SUPERB FAIRY WREN."

"I'M FLORA, YOU CAN CALL ME FLORA. I AM NOT A SUPERB FAIRY WREN AND NO, I WAS NOT WONDERING."

THEY WALKED FARTHER INTO THE *unknown*.
SHE FELT SCARED THAT IT WAS NO LONGER
JUST HER AND THE ROCKS. BUT SHE LIKED
THIS WORLD BETTER.

THEY ARRIVED UPON A MOUSE EATING BERRIES. FLORA GLARED AT IT, AND SAID, "IT MUST BE NICE TAKING WHAT YOU WANT FROM THIS SPECIAL PLACE," HINTING AT HARLIES FERN THEFT.

"BUT LOOK," SAID HARLIE, AND POINTED AT THE ANIMAL NOW MAKING SCAT FILLED WITH LITTLE SEEDS.

"OKAY THAT IS GROSS," SAID FLORA.

"BUT FLORA, THOSE SEEDS WILL GO ON TO GROW INTO MORE BERRY PLANTS. THE PLANTS THAT HELP THE MOUSE SURVIVE NEED HIM TO MULTIPLY TO SURVIVE THEMSELVES! AND EVENTUALLY FEED MORE MICE TOO."

"OH," HOLDING HER NOSE IN THE AIR,
"I STILL THINK THAT'S WEIRD."

HARLIE WENT ON TO SHOW FLORA SOME BEES
AND BUTTERFLIES LANDING ON FLOWERS AND
PICKING UP POLLEN WITH THEIR FURRY
LITTLE BODIES. "THIS WILL HELP THOSE
FLOWERS MAKE MORE FLOWERS AND ALSO
PROVIDE THE NUTRIENTS THOSE FLYING
INVERTEBRATES NEED TO SURVIVE."

SHE TRIED TO STAY UNINTERESTED,
BUT COULD NOT HELP FROM WONDERING.
"WHAT ABOUT THAT BEETLE EATING
THAT TREE? THAT CAN'T BE HELPFUL.
"THAT TREE IS ALREADY DEAD. THE
BEETLE IS TURNING IT INTO A
FERTILE GROWING SURFACE, SO ARE
THOSE."

HE POINTED TO A TROOP OF
MUSHROOMS.

"BUT WHAT ABOUT MY— I MEAN, THE FERN YOU TOOK? HOW WAS THAT USEFUL TO YOU?" HARLIE IGNORED HER.

"SEE THESE ROOTS? THEY TAKE UP WATER FOR THE PLANTS. THERE ARE ALSO TINY FUNGI THAT HELP THEM GET UNDERGROUND NUTRIENTS. THEY ALL LIVE AMONGST THE SOIL, WITH THE MOLES AND THE ANTS AND HAVE THEIR OWN LITTLE WORLD WE CAN'T EVEN SEE."

"UP HERE IN THIS VERY SAME TREE LIVE SQUIRRELS AND BATS AND LEAVES." FLORA BEGAN TO LISTEN CLOSELY. SHE WONDERED ABOUT HOW SHE COULD PLAY A ROLE IN NATURE, TOO. SHE WONDERED WHAT ELSE IN THIS WORLD HAD A SPECIAL, IMPORTANT RELATIONSHIP.

THEY CONTINUED ALONG. SHE SAW PLANTS SOAKING UP SUN, THEN PRODUCING OXYGEN, SHE SAW ANIMALS EATING PLANTS, EVEN ANIMALS EATING OTHER ANIMALS, TO GET ENERGY FOR THEIR DAY. EVERYTHING SEEMED TO BE IN BALANCE AND

flora forgot about her fern.

PART FOUR

FEARS AND
NEW FRONTIERS

WITH A HOP IN HER
STEP, SHE CARRIED
ON WITHOUT
NOTICING THAT
HARLIE WAS NO
LONGER NEXT TO
HER. SHE WANDERED
FARTHER AND
FARTHER INTO THE
WOODS.
FLORA PAUSED TO
ASK A QUESTION,
AND REALIZED
HARLIE WAS
COMPLETELY GONE.
SHE HAD GROWN SO
USED TO HIS
COMPANY AND NOW
FELT LOST WITHOUT
HIM THERE. SHE
BEGAN TO PANIC.

SHE WAS ALONE

"HARLIE? *HARLIE?*" SHE STARTED TO RUN.

THROUGH THICK VINES AND BRANCHES
SHE RAN UNTIL SHE COULDN'T
ANYMORE. SHE STOPPED TO CATCH HER
BREATH AND FOUND HERSELF STARING
INTO THE FACE OF A BEAR.

THE BEAR TOWERED OVER HER. HIS
TEETH WERE SURE TO BE FOR EATING
SMALL GIRLS. HIS PAWS WERE BIGGER
THAN HER HEAD AND HIS CLAWS
REMINDED HER OF THE DEADLY SPIKE
ROCKS FROM HER SIDE OF THE WALL.

SHE WAS FULL OF FEAR, BUT THE BEAR
BARELY EVEN NOTICED SHE EXISTED. SHE
STOOD FROZEN AND NOT SURE WHAT TO DO.
TO HER RELIEF, SHE WAS REMINDED OF THE
MOUSE AS THE BEAR GENTLY PICKED A
BLUEBERRY AND PUT IT UP TO HIS LIPS.
HE WAS NOT OUT TO HURT HER AT ALL!

SHE GAVE HIM A WAVE AND CONTINUED. SHE WAS ONCE AGAIN STOPPED IN HER TRACKS, THIS TIME BY THE MOST BEAUTIFUL TREE SHE HAD EVER SEEN. AND UP IN THE BRANCHES WAS SOMETHING SHE RECOGNIZED . . . . .

her fern!

PART FIVE

FLORA AND THE FERN

FLORA CLIMBED UP THE TREE QUICKLY AND
QUIETLY. SHE WANTED TO GET HER FERN
BACK. WHEN SHE GOT CLOSER SHE SAW
THAT IT WAS WOVEN INTO OTHER THINGS.
IT WAS A NEST FULL OF YOUNG CHARLIE
PARKERS.

THIS WOULD BE THE PERFECT REVENGE, SHE
WOULD TAKE BACK HER FERN ALONG WITH
SOMETHING THAT HARLIE REALLY LOVED.
SHE PLUCKED THE NEST FROM ITS SPOT
AND ESCAPED.

FLORA RAN AND LOOKED DOWN AT THEIR
TINY CHARLIE PARKER FACES TWEETING
UP AT HER. SHE BEGAN TO THINK OF
EVERYTHING HARLIE HAD TAUGHT HER.
SHE TRIPPED AND NOTICED ALSO WOVEN
INTO THE NEST WAS A RIPPED PIECE OF
PAPER, SO SIMILAR TO THE ONE THING
SHE EVER OWNED. SHE TOOK IT OUT AND
HELD IT UP AGAINST HERS. IT FIT.

IT WAS AN ARTICLE FROM AN OLD
NEWSPAPER. COMPLETED IT READ : IT'S ALL
ABOUT FLORA AND FAUNA. IT IS UP TO US
TO PROTECT THE PLANTS AND ANIMALS OF
OUR FORESTS AND SAVE THE PLANET FROM A
GREAT DISASTER!

WHAT HAD SHE DONE? SHE STOLE THESE
BEAUTIFUL BABIES FROM THEIR PARENTS AND
FOR WHAT? ONE LITTLE FERN WHEN SHE WAS
SURROUNDED BY ALL THINGS LIVING? IT WAS
NOT ABOUT HER AT ALL, BUT EVERYTHING PUT
TOGETHER! SO SHE RETURNED, FEELING
GUILTY, BUT EXCITED.

It's all about FLORA and FAUNA

TODAY'S DATE:
NOV. 13, 2015

it is up
to us to
protect the
plants and animals
of our forests and
save the planet from

SHE HOPED HE DIDN'T SEE WHAT SHE TRIED
TO DO, BUT WHEN SHE ARRIVED AT THE
BRANCH SHE TOOK THE NEST FROM, HARLIE
WAS THERE WAITING...

"YOU MADE IT FLORA. I KNEW YOU WOULD DO
THE RIGHT THING."

"SO EVERYTHING YOU TOLD ME, THAT HAD TO
DO WITH THE WORLD BEFORE THE END? THAT'S
HOW THINGS USED TO BE? CAN THEY STAY
THAT WAY NOW?"

HE STARTED TO RESPOND, WHEN A BRANCH
ABOVE BROKE AND BROUGHT THEM BOTH TO
THE GROUND. HARLIE WAS PINNED UNDER IT.

NO,

NO,

NO !

"YOU KNOW WHAT YOU HAVE TO DO FLORA,"
HARLIE WHISPERED WITH HIS LAST
BREATH.

FLORA WANTED TO FLOAT AWAY IN
THE FLOOD OF HER TEARS.

"WHAT DO YOU MEAN I KNOW WHAT TO DO?
YOU CAN'T DIE. THE BABY BIRDS NEED YOU,
THE WORLD NEEDS YOU."
SHE PAUSED, "*I NEED YOU.*"

SHE THEN REACHED INTO HER POCKET AND
PULLED OUT THE SPORE AND PLACED IT
OVER HIM.

"Get some good rest little bird."

AS SHE SAT WITH HIM SHE REMEMBERED
ALL HE HAD TOLD HER ABOUT
EVERYTHING BEING CONNECTED. HER
FROWN FADED AWAY AND SHE WAS AT
PEACE. EVERYTHING WOULD BE OKAY. A
LAST TEAR DROPPED WHERE SHE PLACED
THE SPORE AND SOMETHING STARTED TO
HAPPEN. A FERN EMERGED FROM WHERE
HIS BODY LIE, THEN ANOTHER,
AND THEN A FLOWER...

and then......

"FLORA! FLORA?"

SHE SNAPPED OUT OF A SCIENCE CLASS DAY DREAM.

"ARE YOU LISTENING TO OUR LESSON ON WHY OUR LIVING WORLD IS SO IMPORTANT?"

FLORA REACHED INTO HER POCKET,
PULLED OUT A SPORE
AND SMILED.

THE END.

www.ingramcontent.com/pod-product-compliance
Lightning Source LLC
Chambersburg PA
CBHW060831290526
45792CB00006BB/1887